IMAGES
of America

THE ROSE BOWL

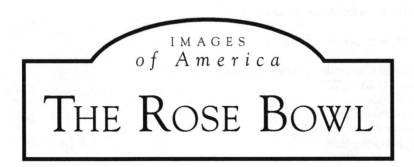

IMAGES
of America

THE ROSE BOWL

Michelle L. Turner and
Pasadena Museum of History

ARCADIA
PUBLISHING

Published by Arcadia Publishing
Charleston, South Carolina

Printed in the United States of America

Library of Congress Control Number: 2009941024

For all general information contact Arcadia Publishing at:
Telephone 843-853-2070
Fax 843-853-0044
E-mail sales@arcadiapublishing.com
For customer service and orders:
Toll-Free 1-888-313-2665

Visit us on the Internet at www.arcadiapublishing.com

In loving memory of Howard and Sally Chewning

CONTENTS

Acknowledgments   6

Introduction   7

1.   The Building of a Bowl   9

2.   The Granddaddy of Them All   25

3.   The Rose Bowl's Grandbaby   45

4.   Rallies and Performances   57

5.   Let's Root for the Home Team   69

6.   The Community's Bowl   81

7.   The International Bowl   93

8.   Other Tracks and Fields   103

9.   The Super Bowl   115

Rose Bowl Scores Since 1923   126

ACKNOWLEDGMENTS

First and foremost, I would like to thank Jeannette O'Malley, executive director of Pasadena Museum of History (PMH), for providing me with the opportunity to write this book. I am also grateful for the additional support of PMH staff members Laura Verlaque and Cedar Phillips, as well as my Arcadia Publishing editor Jerry Roberts. A very special thanks to Bob Bennett, Dr. Lynne Emery, and all of the PMH archives volunteers for their assistance and suggestions. I would also like to express my appreciation to Darryl Dunn, Jess Waiters, Margo Mavridis, Audrey O'Kelley, and everyone at the Rose Bowl Operating Company—thank you for your assistance as well as your stewardship of this remarkable stadium. Thanks are due to Joetta Di Bella at the Tournament of Roses Archives and to everyone in the community who provided photographs for this publication. Finally, I would like to thank my husband, Patrick Edquist, for his support and encouragement, as well as our family, who have now heard countless Rose Bowl anecdotes.

Unless otherwise noted, the photographs reproduced in this book are from the main collection of the archives at Pasadena Museum of History, signified by PMH in the courtesy lines. In addition to the main collection, I relied heavily on the *Pasadena Star-News* Collection (abbreviated PSN), the *Pasadena Star-News* Negatives Collection, the J. Allen Hawkins Collection, and the Tournament of Roses Collection. Photographers and studios are acknowledged when known.

INTRODUCTION

Pasadena is best known for its roses and architecture, both of which are embodied by one structure—the Rose Bowl. Designed by famed Pasadena architect Myron Hunt, the stadium was built specifically for the Tournament of Roses Association's New Year's Day football game. When the bowl was built in 1922 it was considered a remarkable architectural achievement, and it retains that status to this day. Every renovation and upgrade that the stadium has received has been in keeping with Hunt's original design. The structure is a California Historic Civil Engineering Landmark and is listed on the National Register of Historic Places as a National Historic Landmark.

In 1888, a group of Pasadenans formed an elite social club called the Valley Hunt Club. Many of its members had moved to the California town from the Midwest and East Coast because of the favorable climate. At a club meeting, Prof. Charles F. Holder suggested that they hold a festival to show off their new hometown, with its winter roses and oranges, to the rest of the country. The resulting Rose Parade and day of festivities was born in 1890. Since then, the event has continued to grow exponentially. By 1895, the event had grown so large that it was too big for the Valley Hunt Club, and the Tournament of Roses Association was formed with the sole purpose of managing the New Year's Day festival.

Afternoon festivities were held after the parade at the town lot and were moved to Tournament Park in 1900. Various types of events were held, including jousts, footraces, bicycle races, and polo matches. In 1902, the Tournament of Roses Association hosted its first New Year's Day college football game. The next football game was not held until 1916. For several years, *Ben Hur*–inspired chariot races dominated the festivities. When football did return, it came back stronger than before. In 1902, Michigan defeated Stanford 49-0. By 1916, the western universities had teams that could compete on the same level as the eastern teams, and tens of thousands came to see the games. Like the parade that preceded it, the postseason football game continued to become more popular, and the crowds continued to grow larger. The Tournament of Roses Association recognized the need for a larger stadium and began to lay plans for the Rose Bowl.

The Tournament of Roses Association hoped that the game and stadium would become internationally renowned, and in fact, the Rose Bowl has become known around the world. The Rose Bowl game is nicknamed "The Granddaddy of Them All" because it was the first postseason bowl game and remains the most important game in college football to this day. In addition to the New Year's Day game, numerous other sporting events have secured the stadium's place in the history of athletics. The football game inspired the Pasadena Junior Chamber of Commerce to sponsor a Junior Rose Bowl for the junior college leagues. The Rose Bowl has also been the venue for the most important game in professional football—the Super Bowl. Playing host to Olympic events and World Cup finals made the stadium a truly international arena.

The Rose Bowl's field has been transformed throughout the years for other athletic events. In addition to football and soccer, the Rose Bowl has hosted midget car and motocross races, rodeos, track-and-field meets, marathons, bicycle races, and even Frisbee competitions. The pristine football field has been significantly altered for various events only to be restored in time for the New Year's Day game. Yet, no matter what sport, athletic authorities have deemed the stadium and remodeled field a perfect venue. Many of these groups returned to the Rose Bowl for future events.

The large capacity of the bowl has also made it the ideal location for numerous nonathletic events. The Rose Bowl has been used for rallies, concerts, circuses, and other entertainment events. Some of these gatherings have been political or religious in nature. Other activities have been put on at the Rose Bowl for sheer amusement and enjoyment, although even the political rallies often included an entertainment factor. Some of America's greatest bands and entertainers have brought their stages to Pasadena to perform on the Rose Bowl's field. Many of these events, both athletic and nonathletic in nature, have not been put on without objection. Some local residents living in the Arroyo Seco have protested year-round Rose Bowl events. There are also those within the community who believe that the stadium should be used only for football despite the Rose Bowl's long history of playing host to other events.

Since it was built, the stadium has played an important role as a community center for Pasadena. It has held graduation exercises for many Pasadena schools. The size of the stadium allowed for mass graduation ceremonies with spectacular pageantry. Local schools and organizations have used the stadium for various children's events. The Rose Bowl is the home of the largest local flea market, and many residents walk, jog, or bike along the loop surrounding the Rose Bowl. The stadium has provided Pasadena schools with a home football stadium. Three professional soccer teams, including the Los Angeles Galaxy, have also called the stadium home. Beginning in 1982, the Rose Bowl became the home of a university football team when the University of California–Los Angeles (UCLA) Bruins came to Pasadena.

The multipurpose stadium has surpassed its original function to become a historic icon, an ideal arena for any sport or event, and a community center. The stadium in the Arroyo Seco is featured in nearly every advertisement for the city of Pasadena and for good reason. The bowl is utilized for important city events, and major events at the stadium impact the entire city. The Rose Bowl represents more than the Tournament of Roses, sports, and even the Arroyo Seco—it symbolizes the spirit of Pasadena.

One

THE BUILDING OF A BOWL

For years the Tournament of Roses Association relied on temporary solutions to accommodate the growing number of spectators who came to Tournament Park every January. When temporary stands were erected for the 1921 game, it became evident that the festivities had outgrown the venue. W. L. Leishman, president of the Tournament of Roses as well as a contractor, convinced the organization that a bigger, permanent stadium had to be built for the New Year's football game. Leishman continued to work on the project in the years following his presidency. Funding for the bowl was secured after the 1922 game by preselling seats in the future stadium. The Tournament of Roses Association built the stadium on city-owned land in the Arroyo Seco with the agreement that it would lease the property back from the city for 90 days every year.

Famed architect Myron Hunt envisioned the stadium's original design as a horseshoe. It was made a true bowl in 1928 when the south side was enclosed to provide more seating. Since then the stadium has undergone numerous structural improvements and reconstructions. While the Rose Bowl, now under the stewardship of the Rose Bowl Operating Company, is maintained as a state-of-the-art, functioning stadium, it still retains its status as a historical icon.

The 1917 game, and particularly Oregon's victory over Pennsylvania, convinced many easterners that western teams offered good competition. After World War I, the eastern schools continued to send teams to the New Year's Day game. With teams such as Harvard coming to play in Pasadena and the increased popularity of the New Year's Day game, the building of a bowl was inevitable.

Decades before the Rose Bowl was constructed, Henry Biedebach owned a 10-acre ranch on the site of the future stadium. Pictured is Biedebach's family at their Arroyo Seco home. His wife, Sophia Amelia, stands in the center with four of their children—from left to right, Mark, Edward, Rose, and Jacob. After 1921, Henry and Amelia moved to a home on Vernon Street.

Myron Hunt was the architect who designed the new stadium for W. L. Leishman and the Tournament of Roses. When presented with the idea of a stadium in the Arroyo Seco, Hunt stood above the rock-laden land and used a piece of paper with a round cutout to envision the stadium in the suggested location. (Courtesy of the Archives, California Institue of Techology.)

This model shows the original design of the Rose Bowl. Accommodating 57,000 spectators, the new stadium had over 15,000 more seats than Tournament Park. The Tournament of Roses spent $272,198.26 making this model a reality. The Rose Bowl maintained this design for only six years before the seating was expanded.

This photograph shows the work on the stadium is in its early stages, with the tents of the construction workers in the foreground. The photographer would have been standing on the southeast area of the Arroyo looking in a northwesterly direction toward the Linda Vista Hills. Before the construction of the stadium could begin, the trees and brush had to be cleared. (Courtesy of PMH, PSN Collection.)

A *Pasadena Star-News* staff member described the method of construction after taking this photograph. "Concrete forms were placed into position for the tunnels providing access to the sports edifice. The rock-laden earth was then piled up around the tunnels, simultaneously forming the entry way and shaping the rising incline that provided the graduating levels for the three-score or more rows of seats." (Courtesy of PMH, PSN Collection.)

The above photograph shows tunnel 11 along with tunnels 10 and 12 during the early stages of the Rose Bowl's construction. The photograph at right shows the same tunnel almost 60 years later. These concrete tunnels surrounded by rock have become a defining architectural feature of the bowl. Over the years they have remained relatively unchanged, aside from the occasional coat of new paint. (Right, courtesy of PMH, PSN Collection.)

In addition to men and horses, there was some machinery available to make the rocky land ready for a stadium. This photograph, taken on July 5, 1922, shows workers using a steam shovel to manipulate the landscape. A pole for electrical lines can also be seen on the right side of the photograph.

The first section of stands was built at the north end of the stadium. Yet even after this section was completed, many local residents could not decipher the nature of the large new structure in the Arroyo. Note the "stadium" sign that was added to alleviate any confusion. (Courtesy of PMH, PSN Collection.)

These photographs were taken on October 28, 1922, when the first football game took place in the bowl between two Pacific teams—California and the University of Southern California (USC) (who incidentally would also play in the first official Rose Bowl Game against Penn State). Although it was not a New Year's Day game, the event was well attended. In addition to those who purchased seats, the photograph below shows the large number of people who stood at the southern end of the horseshoe to view the game. A few months later, W. L. Leishman predicted that someday the bowl would be "a complete saucer." (Both, courtesy of PMH, Flag Collection.)

This relaxed 1920s scene is in stark contrast to the adrenaline-filled football game that would take place in the same location months later. Note the hedges in the background. Although they were later removed, there are plans to replant the hedges along the edge of the field in 2013. This will allow some fans to walk on the field as they make their way to their seats.

The south side was enclosed in 1928 to provide additional seating. By making the stadium a true bowl, 19,000 more seats were added to the previous seating capacity of 57,000. The cost for this came to $115,000. Enclosing the stadium marked the first of the Rose Bowl's many structural improvements throughout the years.

16

The Pageant of Lights took place in 1929 at the Rose Bowl to commemorate night lighting at the bowl after six steel towers with floodlights were installed around the stadium. The principal dancer, Michio Ito, directed a chorus of women from Pasadena Junior College, whose costumes consisted of colored sateen bodices and white seersucker sleeves and skirts. Two hundred dancers participated in the performance, along with the choruses and an orchestra. The symphonic dance was choreographed to Tchaikovsky's *Andante Cantabile*, two Chopin waltzes, Grieg's *Peer Gynt Suite*, and Dvorak's *New World Symphony*. Ito himself performed his famous Shadow Dance. The performance of the internationally renowned Ito was a unique treat for the 5,000 local residents who attended the show. A few years later, the famous Japanese dancer choreographed *Madame Butterfly* as well as other Hollywood films before returning to Tokyo after the attack on Pearl Harbor, when many Japanese were being forced to leave the United States.

The Rose Bowl continued to get upgrades and improvements throughout the years. Like the enclosing of the bowl in 1928, most of the stadium's upgrades have been made to accommodate more people. In 1931, less than 10 years after the bowl was built, the seating capacity was increased to 86,000 when concrete replaced the wooden section of the stadium. Six years later, 4,000 more seats were added. In 1949, construction crews were called in once again to add additional seating.

These photographs, as well as the ones on the previous page, show various phases of the 1949 project, from the excavation to pouring new concrete. The final result was a seating capacity that reached 100,531. In 1972, the seating was once again increased to 104,696. Although the current official capacity of the Rose Bowl is 92,542, the City of Pasadena and the Rose Bowl Operating Company have found ways to periodically increase the capacity of the stadium. The stadium has held more than 100,000 during some of its biggest games, including Rose Bowl games, a Super Bowl game, an Olympic soccer final, and a UCLA versus USC regular-season game.

To promote the most recent Rose Bowl improvement in 1966, Tournament of Roses member Bill Leishman, grandson of W. L. Leishman, ordered photographs to be taken of the construction site. For this publicity shot, the current Miss Junior Rose Bowl was placed in an open manhole on the field. (Photograph by J. Allen Hawkins; courtesy of PMH, Hawkins Collection.)

The stadium that was originally built solely for the purpose of football got a new track in 1966. After the track was completed, the Rose Bowl played host to track-and-field meets for local Pasadena schools. The Rose Bowl currently does not have a track, and there are no plans to reinstall one. (Photograph by J. Allen Hawkins; courtesy of PMH, Hawkins Collection.)

Here is the Rose Bowl locker room in 1978 prior to the Rose Bowl becoming home to a college football team. The locker rooms were remodeled in 1982 before UCLA came to the stadium. In 2007, the locker rooms were renovated again at the request of UCLA. The almost 28,000-square-foot remodel nearly quadrupled the size of the locker rooms. (Courtesy of PMH, PSN Negatives Collection.)

Another major improvement to the Rose Bowl was the upgrade to the press box in 1992. Built by Perini Building Company, the press box's construction was overseen by project manager John Critelli (pictured at right). As part of an upcoming renovation plan, the capacity of the suites in the press box will increase from 600 to 2,500. (Photograph by Matthew D. Ho; courtesy of PMH, PSN Collection.)

The Yale Bowl was one of the first college football stadiums built in the United States. The bowl, which originally seated more than 70,000 spectators and was completed in 1914, influenced the design of the Rose Bowl. The Rose Bowl Operating Company staff visited the Yale Bowl when it began looking for inspiration for renovations slated to begin in 2011. (Photograph by Darryl Dunn; courtesy of the Rose Bowl Operating Company.)

The iconic stadium that is the focus of the nation on New Year's Day is part of Pasadena's everyday life. Plans to renovate the nearly 90-year-old stadium began in April 2009. The new improvements will upgrade the stadium while acknowledging its historic roots. (Courtesy of PMH, PSN Collection.)

These photographs from 1976 feature (pictured above, from left to right) Tournament of Roses president Carl E. Wopschall, Pasadena mayor Robert Glenn White, and Walter H. Cates and John Howe from the Los Angeles Section of the American Society of Civil Engineers. After admiring the stadium from the aluminum seating that was installed in 1969, the men posed by a plaque commemorating the Rose Bowl's new status as a California Historic Civil Engineering Landmark. A decade later in 1987, the Rose Bowl was placed on the National Register of Historic Places and was designated a National Historic Landmark. (Photographs by Walt Mancini; courtesy of PMH, PSN Collection.)

The photograph above shows the central area of the Arroyo Seco around 1913, almost a decade before the Rose Bowl was built. The canyon was sparsely populated and somewhat barren, but Leishman and Hunt saw the future site of a stadium. Today it is difficult to imagine the Arroyo Seco without the Rose Bowl. The stadium has carved out a place for itself in the canyon, in sports, and in the Pasadena community. In an area with arguably some of the most preeminent architecture in the country, the bowl is truly one of the defining features of the San Gabriel Valley landscape.

Two

THE GRANDDADDY
OF THEM ALL

There is a reason that almost every ticket to a major sporting event held in Pasadena features a red rose—the Pasadena Tournament of Roses. Pasadena's New Year's Day festivities began in 1890 when the Pasadena Valley Hunt Club hosted a parade and games, and the event grew in popularity year after year. In 1895, the annual event had outgrown the Valley Hunt Club, and the Tournament of Roses Association was formed. A town lot, known as Sportsman Park, was the first arena to play host to the events held after the parade, followed by Tournament Park in 1900. The parks held a variety of games, including footraces, jousts, chariot races, and football games. After an earlier attempt in 1902, in 1916, the Tournament of Roses Association decided once again on an annual football game, which proved to be popular—too popular for the small stadium at Tournament Park. Led by W. L. Leishman, the Tournament of Roses Association built the stadium in the Arroyo Seco for the purpose of football.

Since then the stadium that was aptly named the "Rose Bowl" by Tournament of Roses publicist Harlan "Dusty" Hall has played host to an annual championship football game for more than 80 years. Only in 1942, when the threat of foreign attack loomed, was the Tournament of Roses' game played on a different field. Establishing the east versus west matchup had its challenges, but ultimately the Tournament of Roses succeeded in luring the teams from the Big Ten out to Pasadena and in making the New Year's Day postseason game one of the most important games in collegiate football. It has certainly earned the name "The Granddaddy of Them All."

In 1922, Tournament Park held its last New Year's Day game. Although the underdogs from Washington and Jefferson University ultimately held their own against the mighty California, the game was not expected to be that exciting. Nonetheless, a new Tournament of Roses record was made when ticket sales to the game totaled $170,000. The size of the crowd at the game contributed to the decision that a proper bowl had to be built.

W. L. Leishman was a groundbreaking Tournament of Roses president in many ways. As seen above, he was the first president to ride down the parade route in a car rather than in a horse and carriage in 1920. He was also the president who decided that a stadium needed to be built in the Arroyo Seco. His son Lathrop, seen driving the car, became Tournament of Roses president in 1939.

It is not surprising that the cover of the 1923 Tournament of Roses program featured the new stadium with a football player in the foreground. Although the first game in the stadium was actually played the previous October between two California universities, the formal dedication of the Rose Bowl took place on January 1, 1923, when USC took on Penn State for the postseason title. Although improvements and additions continued to be made, the stadium was funded and built in less than a year. The stadium pictured on the program had a field that extended far beyond the south end of the horseshoe. Initially part of the stadium's design, the extension of the field was later abandoned. Since its construction, the Rose Bowl has played host to 88 postseason college football games to date. (Courtesy of PMH, Tournament of Roses Collection.)

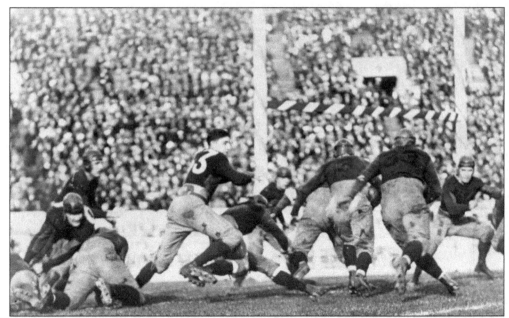

In 1923, USC and Penn State had the honor of playing the first New Year's Day game in the Rose Bowl. In this photograph, USC fullback Joseph Campbell (No. 3) blocks as teammate Roy "Bullet" Baker (No. 33) runs to Penn State's one-yard line. Although the play resulted in three points for Penn State, USC ultimately won the game 14-3.

This packet of postcards for the 1924 Tournament of Roses features the chariot races, which were the main event at Tournament Park on New Year's Day from 1904 to 1915. Although the Tournament of Roses Association never held the races at the Rose Bowl, the revenue from the chariot races helped fund the building of the stadium.

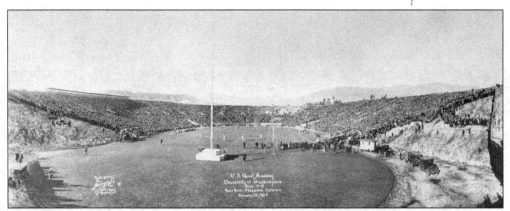

The stadium was still in its original horseshoe shape for the 1924 Rose Bowl game. Only 40,000 spectators witnessed the Navy-Washington game because many tickets were given to a navy fleet that was ordered to sea on December 31, 1923. Although there were plenty of seats available at this game, the attendance during the next few years convinced the Tournament of Roses Association to close off the south end to provide more seating.

It is difficult to imagine that the player charging through the defensive line in this photograph was nicknamed "Sleepy Jim" by his coach, Knute Rockne. Jim Crowley was one of Notre Dame's legendary "Four Horsemen," who won the Rose Bowl game against Stanford in 1925. Crucial to the win, Crowley almost did not play in the game because he and teammate Ed Huntsinger were caught staying out late the night before.

In 1929, California center Roy Riegels played his heart out. He blocked a Georgia Tech punt that led to California captain Irvine Phillips scoring a touchdown. After the game, Georgia Tech center Peter Pund said that Riegels was "the best center I have played against all year. He's a battler, and he never quit." Unfortunately, the thing most people remember of "Wrong Way" Roy Riegels is that he ran the ball down the field for 65 yards in the wrong direction, and that Georgia Tech won the game by one point. Riegels did not realize something was wrong until he was almost at his own goal line. Reigels went on to coach high school and college football after serving in World War II. In 1991, Reigels was inducted into the Rose Bowl Hall of Fame. He was named to California's Hall of Fame in 1998, five years after his death. (Photograph by J. Allen Hawkins.)

The 1939 contest between USC and Duke was one of the closest games in the Rose Bowl's history. After Duke finally kicked a field goal with two minutes left in the game, USC put fourth-string quarterback Doyle Nave and receiver Al Kruger onto the field. With four passes, Nave and Kruger scored a touchdown in what was described by one author as a "movie-like finish." USC won the game 7-3.

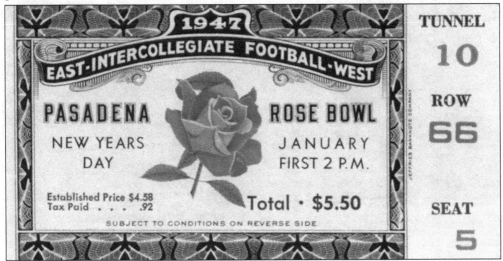

This ticket allowed one lucky spectator to see the first Rose Bowl game between the Pacific Coast Conference (represented by UCLA) and the Big Ten (represented by Illinois). Note that the cost of the ticket was $5.50. Today a devoted fan may pay a few hundred dollars for a ticket to "The Granddaddy of Them All." (Courtesy of PMH, Tournament of Roses Collection.)

Although not obvious in this photograph, it rained throughout the day on January 1, 1955. Despite the weather, both USC and Ohio State played hard in what was described by *Times* reporter Braven Dyer as "waterlogged lunatics." The stadium was filled with fans despite the rain, and Ohio State won the game 20-7. (Courtesy of PMH, PSN Negatives Collection.)

In this photograph, University of Washington's Brent Wooten tackles Wisconsin's Ronald Steiner near the 10-yard line during the 1960 Rose Bowl. Washington went on to beat Wisconsin 44-8. Wisconsin had also lost its only previous Rose Bowl game to USC. The team would go on to win three Rose Bowls decades later in 1994, 1999, and 2000. (Courtesy of PMH, PSN Negatives Collection.)

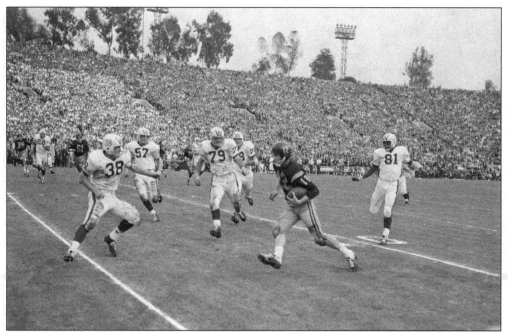

Quarterback Pete Beathard's record-setting performance in 1963 led the Trojans to their 10th Rose Bowl victory. Although the final score was USC 42, Wisconsin 37, Wisconsin had outgained USC by 119 yards. Badgers' quarterback Ron VanderKelen set his own record with 33 completions. (Courtesy of PMH, PSN Negatives Collection.)

Although USC lost the 1967 game to Purdue 14-13, many in the crowd must have been excited to see a local boy come home to play on New Year's Day. USC right halfback Rod Sherman had played for Muir High School, which used the Rose Bowl as its home field. (Courtesy of PMH, PSN Negatives Collection.)

At the 1973 Rose Bowl, USC quarterback Sam Cunningham scored four touchdowns and led the Trojans to a 42-27 victory over Ohio State. Everyone on the USC team was at his best that day. Lynn Swan (No. 22) and Charles Young (No. 89) both caught six passes each during the course of the game. (Courtesy of PMH, PSN Negatives Collection.)

At the 1975 Rose Bowl Game, USC tailback Anthony Davis was injured and led off the field by coaches. This was the third consecutive Rose Bowl that Davis played in against Ohio State. USC and Ohio State have competed on numerous occasions for the Rose Bowl game trophy, playing each other seven times to date. (PMH, PSN Negatives Collection)

Going into the 1977 Rose Bowl game, Michigan thought they had a good chance to win. The president of USC, Dr. John R. Hubbard, was not too worried, joking, "A horse is a helluva lot faster than a wolverine." Trojan placekicker Art Sorce and the rest of the USC team proved their president right, winning the game 14-6. (Courtesy of PMH, PSN Negatives Collection.)

The Wolverines got another chance at the Rose Bowl in 1978. In this photograph, Michigan's John Anderson kicks the ball as Washington's Dick Knudson (No. 14) and Jim Pence (No. 18) close in. Michigan lost the game 27-20. The Wolverines and Huskies met again in 1981, with Michigan coming out ahead 23-6. The two teams have played each other four times to date, each winning twice. (Courtesy of PMH, PSN Negatives Collection.)

The sixth New Year's Day game between USC and Ohio State in 1980 was one of the closest games in Rose Bowl history, with USC barely coming out on top 17-16. In the background of this photograph of USC's Herb Ward, the crowd is on their feet cheering at the exciting game. (Courtesy of PMH, PSN Negatives Collection.)

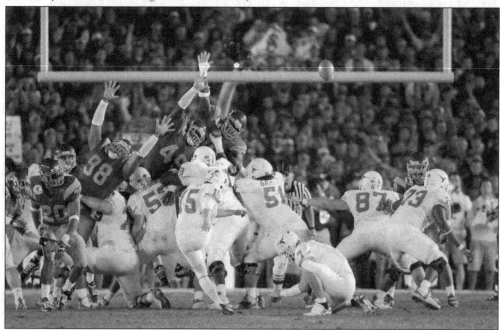

On January 7, 2010, the Rose Bowl played host to its third Bowl Championship Series (BSC) National Championship game. Two prior games in 2002 and 2006 doubled as both the Rose Bowl and the BSC Championship. Pictured is the 2006 dual championship between the Texas Longhorns and the USC Trojans. (Courtesy of the Tournament of Roses Archives.)

Pictured from left to right are four inductees into the Rose Bowl Hall of Fame: Fred "Curly" Morrison was Ohio's State's Rose Bowl MVP in 1950, O. J. Simpson completed an 80-yard touchdown run for USC in 1969, Bo Schembechler was a coach for University of Michigan and took his team to the Rose Bowl 10 times, and Bob Stiles was Rose Bowl Player of the Game in 1966. (Photograph by Nancy Newman-Bauer; courtesy of PMH, PSN Collection.)

For the University of Washington team, the slow-paced parade must have stood in stark contrast to the hard-fought game they played afterward in the Rose Bowl. Both Washington and the Naval Academy had injured players carried off of the field, and Washington kicker Les Sherman managed two conversions with a broken toe. The final score of the brutal 1924 Rose Bowl game was 14-14. (Courtesy of PMH, Flag Collection.)

52nd
Annual

Rose Bowl
Kick-Off
Luncheon

SPONSORED BY THE KIWANIS CLUB OF PASADENA

Part of the Rose Bowl tradition is the Kick-Off Luncheon held every year; however, the Tournament of Roses does not sponsor this event. For many years, the Kiwanis Club of Pasadena, another local community group, sponsored the luncheon. South Pasadena High School also participated in 1981 by having its band perform at the event.

Although the Tournament of Roses Association is charged with putting on "The Granddaddy of Them All," other community organizations also help prepare for the event. Here Phil Ishizu, a volunteer with the Pasadena Jaycees as well as the owner of Sunnyslope Gardens, supervises the colorization of the Rose Bowl field just days before January 1. (Photograph by Nancy Newman-Bauer; courtesy of PMH, PSN Collection.)

There are more than 100 varieties of rose bushes on the Rose Bowl property between the stadium and the fence. Although the stadium has a large gardening staff to care for its numerous plants, for a time the local community came to the stadium to help. The above photograph, taken on January 25, 1988, features members of the Pasadena Rose Society pruning the rose bushes that surround the Rose Bowl. The Rose Queen and her court were also in attendance at the event. These photographs ran in the *Pasadena Star-News* with the caption "It's that time again." (Photographs by John Lloyd; courtesy of PMH, PSN Collection.)

In 1979, USC played Michigan in the Rose Bowl. In addition to more practice on the field, players had to prepare for the big day by participating in the Rose Bowl photograph day. Pictured from left to right are USC players Charles White, Paul McDonald, Lynn Cain, Calvin Sweeney, and Kevin Williams. (Courtesy of PMH, PSN Negatives Collection.)

In addition to the grand marshal, the Rose Court also attends the big game after the New Year's Day parade. Pictured is Rose Queen Barbara Hewitt arriving with her court at the Rose Bowl on January 2, 1967 (January 1 was on a Sunday that year). (Courtesy of PMH, PSN Negatives Collection.)

Grand marshals Roy Rogers and Dale Evans, husband and wife, presided over the 1977 game between USC and Michigan. Here the two Western stars speak at a press conference for the big game. Although the long list of grand marshals also includes politicians and heroes, the majority have been from the entertainment industry. (Courtesy of PMH, PSN Negatives Collection.)

Walt Disney served as the Tournament of Roses' grand marshal in 1966. Here he is, with his wife, Lillian, but without Mickey Mouse, entering the stadium after the parade. It is tradition for the grand marshal to flip the coin at the beginning of the Rose Bowl game. UCLA beat Michigan State 14-12 to win its first Rose Bowl in the game Disney presided over.

This photograph from November 1961 shows Pasadena mayor Jo Heckman with Buck Warren. The artist carved the 13.5-ton, 36-inch-tall rose sculpture seen in the background out of redwood. The iconic symbol of New Year's Day in Pasadena served as a giant reminder of the excitement to come. (Photograph by Ed Norgord; courtesy of PMH, PSN Collection.)

The Rose Bowl always promises to be a good game, and every diehard college football fan tunes in or shows up to watch. However, New Year's Day in Pasadena is not just about the gridiron; it is also about the spectacle. Pictured are doves that were released from the stadium before USC took on Ohio State in 1980. (Courtesy of PMH, PSN Negatives Collection.)

Although the Washington Huskies played a good game against the Minnesota Gophers at the 1961 Rose Bowl, most people remember it as the year of the Great Rose Bowl Hoax. A group of Caltech students, known as the "Fiendish Fourteen," modified Washington's halftime card show for the crowd to display the Caltech beaver and then the word "Caltech" itself. This was not the last prank played by Caltech students at a Rose Bowl game. In 1984, two Caltech students modified the electronic scoreboard to display Caltech and MIT as the competing teams rather than the actual competing teams—Illinois and UCLA. (Both, California Institute of Technology.)

In 1950, the Tournament of Roses' Rose Bowl game trophy went to Ohio State, who had won against the representative of the newly formed Athletic Association of Western Universities, the University of California. Also know as the Leishman Trophy, this sterling silver masterpiece is produced by Tiffany and Company. (Courtesy of PMH, Hawkins Collection.)

The tunnels are barely visible among the throngs of people who filled the stadium to watch the Minnesota-UCLA Rose Bowl game in 1962. Nearly 100,000 fans filled the stadium, making gate receipts surpass $1 million. With few exceptions, the Rose Bowl game has always been played to sold-out crowds. (Courtesy of PMH, PSN Negatives Collection.)

Three

THE ROSE BOWL'S
GRANDBABY

From 1946 to 1977, the Rose Bowl intermittently played host to the Junior Rose Bowl, also known as the "Grandbaby of the Rose Bowl." Unlike the Rose Bowl, which features a western team that can come from California, Washington, Oregon, or Arizona, the Junior Rose Bowl always had a California representative. This postseason game pitted the California Junior College champion against the champion from the National Junior College Athletic Association (NJCAA). Often the California team was fairly local; participants included the junior colleges from Pasadena, Long Beach, Compton, and Santa Ana. This made the Junior Rose Bowl a uniquely local and national postseason game.

The Pasadena Junior Chamber of Commerce, who hosted various events to go along with the game, sponsored the bowl. Many of the New Year's Day Rose Bowl traditions were carried over to the Junior Rose Bowl. Each year a Miss Junior Rose Bowl was chosen, and she was sometimes referred to as the Junior Rose Bowl Queen. And, of course, there was always a parade down Colorado Boulevard. The Jaycees also chose a charity each year that would benefit from the tickets sales, and tickets could be purchased at various stores and organizations around Pasadena, including Vroman's Bookstore. This "baby" bowl game had local support as well as national appeal. At its height, the Junior Rose Bowl was ranked as the fifth-largest bowl game in the country.

OFFICIAL PROGRAM

$.4836 Selling Price
.0164 Sales Tax
TOTAL PRICE

50¢

Tenth Annual

JUNIOR ROSE BOWL GAME

SPONSORED BY PASADENA JUNIOR CHAMBER OF COMMERCE

Jones Junior College
ELLISVILLE, MISSISSIPPI
VS.
Compton College
COMPTON, CALIFORNIA

SATURDAY, DECEMBER 10, 1955 — 1:30 P.M.

In 1955, Compton College went up against the Bobcats from Mississippi in the 10th Junior Rose Bowl. As part of the 10-year anniversary celebration, Junior Rose Bowl founders Myron Thomas, Walter Hoefflin, P. H. "Puss" Halbriter, and Bill Schroeder were the day's grand marshals. Football fans were also excited about the game because the Jones County team was considered the best in the nation—outside of California. The 57,132 people in the crowd set an attendance record for the Junior Rose Bowl for the next two decades. The anticipation leading up to the game was doubtlessly heightened by the various football VIPs who had come to show their support. At a luncheon before the game, Jordan Oliver, the coach of Yale's football team, said that the Junior Rose Bowl was "the second biggest bowl game in the country." Compton College won the 1955 championship 22-13.

Long Beach City College took on Cameron College of Lawton, Oklahoma, in the 1964 Junior Rose Bowl Game. The team from Oklahoma was so focused that they skipped the traditional trip to Disneyland in favor of more practice time. Despite their dedication, Cameron College lost to Long Beach 28-6. (Photograph by J. Allen Hawkins; courtesy of PMH, Hawkins Collection.)

The 1966 Junior Rose Bowl was an exciting year for Pasadena because the Lancers of Pasadena City College (PCC) were back in the game. Journalist Don Pickard reported that "fans are starting to get excited again" as the game between PCC and Henderson County Junior College of Texas neared. Although PCC lost to Henderson 40-13, the team was still the Western State Conference champions. (Photograph by J. Allen Hawkins; courtesy of PMH, Hawkins Collection.)

In 1968, Sacramento State College represented California against Grambling College of Louisiana (now Grambling State University). This artistic rendering of a photograph taken by professional photographer J. Allen Hawkins was probably used for marketing purposes because it was a good action shot of the game. The 1968 game was unique in that it was one of two Junior Rose Bowls to feature two teams from the National Collegiate Athletic Association (NCAA) college division. (Photograph by J. Allen Hawkins; courtesy of PMH, Hawkins Collection.)

Jerry Graves, pictured here in 1965, was chairman of the Junior Rose Bowl Committee. His commitment to the game was so strong that the *Pasadena Star-News* joked that he would do a rain-prevention dance before the game to try to ensure good weather for the December matchup. (Photograph by J. Allen Hawkins; courtesy of PMH, Hawkins Collection.)

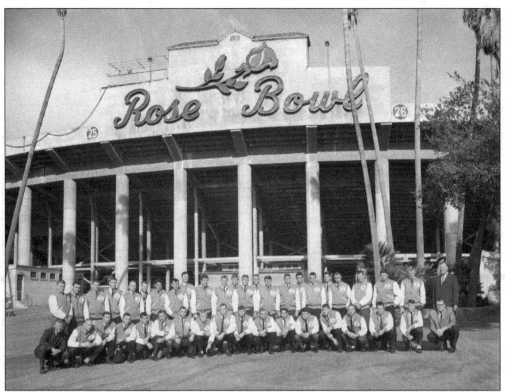

One tradition that carried over from the Rose Bowl to the Junior Rose Bowl was picture day. In 1963, the eastern representative from Oklahoma posed outside of the south end of the Rose Bowl. Oklahoma, who sent another football team the following year, became very familiar with Junior Rose Bowl traditions. (Photograph by J. Allen Hawkins; courtesy of PMH, Hawkins Collection.)

Another Junior Rose Bowl tradition was the airport arrival. Every year a delegation from Pasadena, which of course included Miss Junior Rose Bowl, went to the airport to greet the visiting eastern team. The team from Oklahoma, pictured in 1964, also attended a Quarterback Club annual luncheon at the Huntington Sheraton Hotel. (Photograph by J. Allen Hawkins; courtesy of PMH, Hawkins Collection.)

No matter how good the teams were and no matter how important the game, the bands scheduled to perform and the subsequent musical spectacle were always discussed in the sports section of the *Pasadena Star-News* and usually in the event's program as well. During the 1964 halftime show, the bands formed the words "Jr Rose Bowl" on the field. (Photograph by J. Allen Hawkins; courtesy of PMH, Hawkins Collection.)

These flag and song girls were practicing for the 1949 Junior Rose Bowl game, which was between the teams from Santa Ana and Little Rock. Normally a much-appreciated presence at any game, these women needed to do little to excite the crowd that night. The nearly 34,000 fans anxiously watched as Arkansas became the first eastern team to win a Junior Rose Bowl, with a final score of 25-19. (Photograph by J. Allen Hawkins; courtesy of PMH, Hawkins Collection.)

On December 11, 1976, the second to last Junior Rose Bowl took place in Pasadena, and enthusiasm and excitement ran high among the football community as Ellsworth Community College from Iowa Falls, Iowa, (above) went up against Bakersfield College (below). It was anybody's game, and even many sports analysts would not choose a favorite. Most were simply happy to see the championship revived once again after it had been discontinued in 1966. Both coaches told the *Pasadena Star-News* "that the game was good for junior college football and junior college athletics in general." A California team took the final title, with Bakersfield winning the game 29-14. Pasadena City College would take the final Junior Rose Bowl title in 1977. (Both, courtesy of PMH, PSN Negatives Collection.)

The junior colleges may not have a queen and princesses, but they do have Miss Junior Rose Bowl. Although not part of the Tournament of Roses, in this 1966 photograph Donna Edwards is reminiscent of a Rose Queen with her white suit and roses. (Photograph by J. Allen Hawkins; courtesy of PMH, Hawkins Collection.)

Bob Hope was grand marshal of the Rose Parade in 1947 and in 1969, but in 1960, he also participated in the Junior Rose Bowl by posing for a photo op with Miss Junior Rose Bowl Joan Zeman. In the photograph, Miss Junior Rose Bowl is giving tickets for the charity game to the entertainer/philanthropist. (Photograph by J. Allen Hawkins; courtesy of PMH, Hawkins Collection.)

Every year the Junior Rose Bowl benefited a charitable cause. In 1960, the money raised went to help children with cerebral palsy. The fund-raiser was bound to be a success since the Jaycee game had become the fifth-largest bowl game in the country. (Photograph by J. Allen Hawkins; courtesy of PMH, Hawkins Collection.)

In addition to celebrities like Bob Hope, Miss Junior Rose Bowl also gave tickets to notable Pasadenans such as the coach of the Pasadena City College football team, Don Hunt. Although the Lancers were not in the 1965 game these tickets were for, they made a surprise comeback the following season and played in the 1966 Junior Rose Bowl. (Photograph by J. Allen Hawkins; courtesy of PMH, Hawkins Collection.)

A major postseason football game at the Rose Bowl was always preceded by a parade through Pasadena, regardless of whether or not the game was on New Year's Day. These unidentified women and their Dodge convertibles were entrants in the 1964 Junior Rose Bowl Parade. (Photograph by J. Allen Hawkins; courtesy of PMH, Hawkins Collection.)

The competing junior colleges were not the only parade participants. San Marino High School's band marched in the 1963 parade. While the stands in the background were reserved for the New Year's Day parade a couple of weeks later, many residents gathered on sidewalks and balconies to view the Junior Rose Bowl festivities. (Photograph by J. Allen Hawkins; courtesy of PMH, Hawkins Collection.)

Hollywood starlet Barbara Bates, seen here with an admiring fan, attended a dance that was held at the civic auditorium to commemorate the second-annual Junior Rose Bowl in 1947. The dance was part of a series of events that took place in mid-December around the time of the game. In addition to the parade and dance, there was also a luncheon, a trip to Disneyland, and, after the game, a victory party. (Photograph by J. Allen Hawkins; courtesy of PMH, Hawkins Collection.)

Orange Coast College celebrated at a victory party after the 1963 Junior Rose Bowl when they beat Northeastern Oklahoma 21-0. Another Oklahoma team, from Cameron College, came to Pasadena the following year to try to claim the Junior Rose Bowl title. (Photograph by J. Allen Hawkins; courtesy of PMH, Hawkins Collection.)

In addition to the Junior Rose Bowl, the Pasadena Junior Chamber of Commerce also sponsored another annual event at the Rose Bowl—the Football Circus. Like the Junior Rose Bowl, the Football Circus was a local fund-raiser. It was a full day of football with approximately 300 boys playing flag football. Participating teams came from Eliot Junior High School, La Canada Junior High School, Marshall Junior High School, McKinley Junior High School, Washington Junior High School, and Wilson Junior High School. The B-teams from Muir High School and Pasadena High School also took part in the fund-raiser. In addition, the festivities included entertainment by the school bands and cheer squads. (Photographs by J. Allen Hawkins; courtesy of PMH, Hawkins Collection.)

Four

RALLIES AND
PERFORMANCES

The sheer size of the Rose Bowl has made it the perfect venue for some of the most significant gatherings that have taken place in Southern California. For this reason, the stadium has seen thousands upon thousands enter the Rose Bowl stands, and even the field, to join together for a common belief. The Rose Bowl played host to some of the most significant religious and peace rallies of the 20th century, notably the antinuclear peace rallies in the 1980s.

The Rose Bowl has also seen some of the largest nonathletic entertainment events in the area. The annual fireworks show is a Pasadena tradition and draws tens of thousands each year. Numerous musical groups have chosen the Rose Bowl for their Southern California tour dates, including Guns N' Roses, the Eagles, and *NSYNC. In 2009, U2 and the Black Eyed Peas set a new concert attendance record of 97,000 for the Rose Bowl. Michael Jackson performed at the stadium for the 1993 Super Bowl. In addition to bands, other entertainments, such as circuses, have chosen the venue in hopes of attracting large crowds.

In June 1982, the Rose Bowl began playing host to antinuclear peace concerts. At this "Peace Sunday" concert on June 17 an estimated 80,000 people filled the Rose Bowl. The rallies were spurred by the Second Special Session of the United Nations on Disarmament. Similar concerts took place in other cities across the county, including in San Francisco and New York. (Photograph by John Lloyd; courtesy of PMH, PSN Collection.)

Those showing the peace sign at Peace Sunday could have been moved to do so by a song, a speech, or a prayer. Bob Dylan, Stevie Wonder, and Don Felder and Timothy Schmidt of the Eagles were among the musicians at the event. Speakers included Jane Fonda, Rev. Jesse Jackson, and U.S. president Ronald Reagan's daughter Patti Davis. Numerous celebrities came to the Rose Bowl to promote peace. (Photograph by Blake Sell; courtesy of PMH, PSN Collection.)

In a *Pasadena Star-News* article, journalist Kathy Braidhill described the large crowd as a group that "hailed from all races, religions and ages, protesting nuclear weapons in 80s style with rock music, prayer and anti-nuclear speakers." To Braidhill, these peace rallies seemed to be embraced by a wider range of society compared to the peace movement of the 1960s. The attendance of the diverse group was so high at the first Peace Sunday at the Rose Bowl that a second event was quickly organized. One of the attendees at the peace concerts was local Altadena resident Timothy Dundon, appearing as his alter ego "Zeke the Sheik." Although never elected to public office, the self-proclaimed "guru of doo-doo" is known throughout the community for his use of permaculture compost. Zeke the Sheik also participates in Pasadena's Doo-Dah Parade. (Photograph by John Lloyd; courtesy of PMH, PSN Collection.)

César Chávez is best known for leading the labor movement for California migrant farmworkers, but he was also involved with other important causes. In 1989, Chávez came to the Rose Bowl to speak at a gathering for the Nuclear Weapons Freeze Campaign. (Copyright © 2010 by Victor Aleman. This photograph is published with permission 2MUN-DOS.com Collection.)

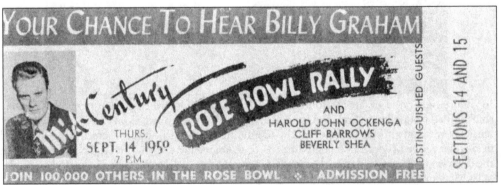

In 1950, Fuller Seminary's publicist Carl Henry coordinated a rally for evangelist Billy Graham. The rally was considered a success by most, but Henry was disappointed. Although the ticket reads "Join 100,000 others at the Rose Bowl," only 50,000 attended the rally. In fact, the rally launched Graham's career, and he returned to the Rose Bowl in 2004 for his Greater Los Angeles Crusade.

When this photograph was taken in 1935, the Pasadena Fire Department had been putting on a circus and fireworks show at the Rose Bowl for nearly a decade. Revenue from the Fourth of July show would then go to the Fireman's Band Fund, which supported local firemen and Pasadena's fire stations. The fire department continued to organize the circus and fireworks show until 1981. The popularity of the show has not diminished, and the Rose Bowl Operating Company continues to host an annual Fourth of July celebration and fireworks show. The full day of festivities begins around 2:00 p.m. and continues for seven and a half hours, until the evening is concluded with a spectacular fireworks show that lasts approximately half an hour. The show has been the center of Pasadena's Fourth of July celebrations for more than eight decades.

Just like the Tournament of Roses, the Pasadena Fire Department liked to outdo themselves year after year. More than two decades after the Fourth of July festivities were inaugurated, the fireworks show still amazed the crowd, and it was guaranteed to only get better. The program from 1956 boasts that the show would include "the first display in Southern California of Rainbow Waters augmented by fireworks."

The 1986 Fourth of July Rose Bowl celebration was also the final ceremony commemorating Pasadena's centennial. Before the fireworks display that featured replicas of city hall's dome and the Statue of Liberty, trombonist Al Jenkins and the rest of the Don Heaston Band performed. (Photograph by John Lloyd; courtesy of PMH, PSN Collection.)

This photograph was taken on July 3, 1992. These members of Mexitlan, a dance group from Highland Park, are practicing for Americafest the next day. In addition to traditional clowns, the Rose Bowl Fourth of July celebration now includes various types of performances, including dance troops, drum corps, and gymnastics. (Photograph by Jonathan Alcorn; courtesy of PMH, PSN Collection.)

Even with all of the various types of performances that had been added to the Fourth of July celebration throughout the years, clowns remained an entertainment mainstay decades after the original Fourth of July show began. This photograph shows Heide Karp entertaining the crowd with a large ball at the 1986 Rose Bowl circus show. (Photograph by Barrett Stinson; courtesy of PHM, PSN Collection.)

After the Osmonds singing group refused to perform at the 1984 Fourth of July celebration, the Los Angeles Olympic Organizing Committee became one of the new sponsors of the event. To salute the Olympics, the LA Lights Rhythmic Gymnastic team performed a routine that introduced the crowd to the new Olympic event. The photograph below features Cara Walker performing rhythmic gymnastics using a long silk ribbon. Adding a gymnastics component to the program allowed local residents to see the sport at the Rose Bowl even though the gymnastic Olympic events held that same summer were at a different venue in Los Angeles. (Photographs by John Lloyd; courtesy of PMH, PSN Collection.)

Most years, between 40,000 and 50,000 people converge at the Rose Bowl for its annual Fourth of July celebration. Since one-third of the stadium's seats are unavailable due to safety concerns, the crowd effectively fills up the Rose Bowl. In addition, thousands more gather in Brookside Park, on nearby streets, and line Colorado Street Bridge to view the fireworks show. (Courtesy of PMH, PSN Collection.)

These bathing suit–wearing women are promoting the Water Follies and Ice-arama performance that took place at the Rose Bowl over Labor Day weekend in 1969. Three large water tanks were brought in for the swimmers and ice-skaters. The *Pasadena Star-News* joked that it was the first time water follies had taken place in the stadium since the 1955 Rose Bowl, when the game was almost rained out. (Photograph by J. Allen Hawkins; courtesy of PMH, Hawkins Collection.)

Two circuses came to the Rose Bowl in 1953. One was the famous Ringling Brothers and Barnum and Bailey Circus and the other was the Black Brothers Circus. Whereas the large Ringling Brothers act was restricted to the Rose Bowl parking lot, the Black Brothers performed in the actual stadium. (Photograph by J. Allen Hawkins; courtesy of PMH, Hawkins Collection.)

New Year's Day was not the only day of the year that decorated cars made their way down the streets of Pasadena; however, this car was not bound for the Rose Parade but for the Rose Bowl. In 1995, Charles Hunt Jr. drove out in this transformed four-door Mercury to see the Eagles concert. (Photograph by Hope Frazier; courtesy of PMH, PSN Collection.)

Half of the experience of attending any sports event or concert at the Rose Bowl is picnicking in Brookside Park or tailgating in the Rose Bowl parking lot. Even as it starts to rain, Eagles fan Skip Mack cooks chili on top of his car. (Photograph by Cindy Darby; courtesy of PMH, PSN Collection.)

When the Eagles' reunion tour finally came to the Rose Bowl in January 1995, the concertgoers accepted the winter weather. As Keith Sharon put it, "When you've waited this long for hell to freeze over, it's going to take more than cold weather and a little rain to keep you away." These fans are enjoying a short break in the rain. (Photograph by Cindy Darby; courtesy of PMH, PSN Collection.)

In 1993, the stadium experienced something that was a first in Super Bowl history—more television viewers watched the halftime show than the game itself. The performance of Michael Jackson, seen here rehearsing, was expected to be so popular that other television networks did not even bother broadcasting counterprogramming. Ninety-one million viewers watched Michael Jackson perform at the Rose Bowl. (Photograph by Chou Ching Yeh; courtesy of PMH, PSN Collection.)

In 2009, the Rose Bowl hosted its biggest concert to date—U2. Ninety-seven thousand fans came to the Rose Bowl to see the band's only California performance of its 360 Tour. This photograph shows the top of the alien-like stage that was brought in for the performance. (Courtesy of Bill Warren.)

Five

LET'S ROOT FOR THE HOME TEAM

Although the Rose Bowl was built for the Tournament of Roses game held every January, the stadium has a long history of playing host to local football games during the regular season. Since 1982, the stadium has been the home of the UCLA football team. And even before the Bruins came to Pasadena, the Rose Bowl held the home games of most of the local teams. These school teams would use the stadium as their home field during the same season, making the Rose Bowl one of the busiest football stadiums in Southern California. These regular-season games brought the community to the stadium, particularly the much-anticipated annual Turkey Tussle between Pasadena High School and John Muir High School.

In addition to football, the Rose Bowl has also been the home field to several Los Angeles soccer teams. The Los Angeles Aztecs, the short-lived Los Angeles Wolves, and the Los Angeles Galaxy have all called the Rose Bowl home.

Pasadenans could continue to cheer on many young athletes after they left Pasadena and the Rose Bowl field. Ray Bartlett, seen playing for UCLA in 1940, had played for Pasadena City College before becoming a Bruin. Bartlett later returned to Pasadena and was active in the police department and city government. (Courtesy of PMH, Black History Collection.)

Southern California's biggest collegiate rivalry is between USC and UCLA. This 1975 game was played at the Los Angeles Memorial Coliseum, but it led to a trip to Pasadena for the Bruins. After winning the game, UCLA went on to beat Ohio State at the Rose Bowl 23-10. The next time UCLA would play in the Rose Bowl, they would play as the home team in 1982. (Courtesy of PMH, PSN Negatives Collection.)

70

In the fall of 1982, the City of Pasadena Management Association welcomed the Rose Bowl's new home team, the UCLA Bruins, to the stadium. Prior to the Rose Bowl, UCLA played at the Los Angeles Memorial Coliseum. The Bruins still play at the Coliseum every other year to play their archrivals, the USC Trojans. (Courtesy of PMH, PSN Collection.)

After a successful first season at the Rose Bowl, UCLA played in the 1983 Rose Bowl game. It was the 60th anniversary of the Rose Bowl game at the stadium. UCLA won the game against Michigan 24-14. The teams played in front of a packed crowd, with nearly 105,000 spectators in attendance. (Courtesy of PMH, PSN Collection.)

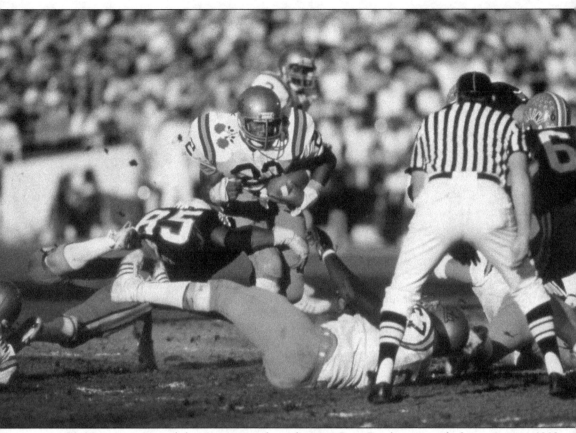

The Bruins continued the momentum from the 1983 Rose Bowl game, and after a winning 1983 regular season, they went on to play in the Rose Bowl game for a second consecutive year. And for the second year in a row, UCLA earned the championship title after winning the game against Illinois 45-9. The two teams had met before in the 1947 Rose Bowl game, when Illinois won 45-14. The UCLA players are wearing their white road jerseys because, technically, the Bruins were the "visiting team" for the postseason game. Note the roses on the jersey of UCLA fullback Bryan Wiley. This game is also remembered for the scoreboard prank that was played on the crowd by a couple of Caltech students. The game marked the 70th Rose Bowl game played since 1902. (Courtesy of Tournament of Roses Archives.)

Since making the Rose Bowl their home stadium, the Bruins have played in five postseason Rose Bowl games to date. In 1994, the Bruins played the Wisconsin Badgers. Pictured is UCLA free safety Marvin Goodwin (No. 22) attempting to tackle Wisconsin running back Terrell Fletcher (No. 41). Wisconsin won the game 21-16. (Courtesy of Tournament of Roses Archives.)

With the UCLA football team came "The Solid Gold Sound," also known as the UCLA Bruins marching band. The band has performed at the Rose Bowl for many UCLA-USC matchups over the years. Here the band energizes the crowd at a game against archrival USC in 2006. The UCLA and USC bands also competed in their own "Band Bowl." (Courtesy of Benjamin Chua.)

UCLA was the first university to employ the Rose Bowl as their home field, but they were not the first college. Decades before the Bruins came to Pasadena, the Arroyo stadium was home to the football teams from John Muir Tech Junior College and Pasadena City College. This photograph is from Muir's 1943 season when they played the junior college from East Los Angeles.

The Los Angeles Wolves were the area's soccer team from 1966 to 1968. After the end of a successful year at the Los Angeles Memorial Coliseum, the team became one of the founding members of the North American Soccer League and played their home games at the Rose Bowl. The franchise did not survive to see another season in Pasadena, and in 1969, the Wolves moved to the Midwest. (Anonymous.)

The Los Angeles Aztecs were a soccer team that competed against other American and Canadian teams from 1974 to 1981, with the Rose Bowl as their home field from 1978 to 1980. Here is the team in 1980 preparing for practice. Although the league was confined to North America, the Los Angeles team had players from 17 different countries. (Courtesy of PMH, PSN Negatives Collection.)

The Rose Bowl was home to the Los Angeles Galaxy soccer team for seven years, until the team moved to the Home Depot Center in Carson in 2003. On August 1, 2009, the team came back to the Rose Bowl in a big way when the world's most famous soccer player, David Beckham, came to Pasadena with the Galaxy to play FC Barcelona. (Photograph by Robert Mercado; courtesy of the Rose Bowl Operating Company.)

By the 1960s, the annual Turkey Tussle was a Pasadena tradition. Pasadena High School (PHS) and Muir High School had been playing the game for years, but the 10,000-strong crowd that came to see the 1962 tussle witnessed a first—a PHS victory. The Bulldogs won the game 21-14 in the last 43 seconds. (Courtesy of PMH, PSN Negatives Collection.)

November 15, 1975, was a big day in high school football for the West San Gabriel Valley. There were three big games that day: a CIF playoff game, the Foothill League finals, and the Turkey Tussle, which was played at the Rose Bowl. Largely because of their breakaway ability, Pasadena won the Turkey Tussle 35-14. The Rose Bowl win made Pasadena High School cochampions of the Pacific League, with Arcadia High School. (Courtesy of PMH, PSN Negatives Collection.)

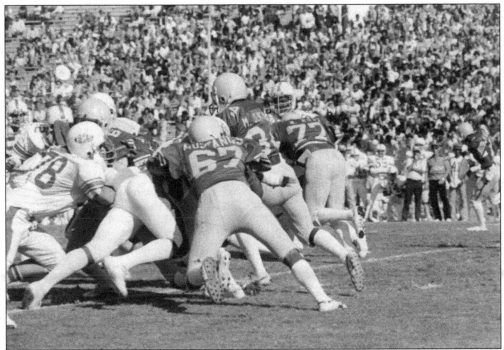

In November 1977, the Bulldogs and the Mustangs met at the Rose Bowl once again for the 30th Turkey Tussle. The game took Pasadena High School out of the playoffs and made Muir High School the Coastal Conference cochampions with Arcadia High School. It also marked the 100th victory for Muir coach Jim Brownfield. (Courtesy of PMH, PSN Negatives Collection.)

Embree Buses, located at 303 North Allen Avenue, was the company used by all local schools. These buses were used to transport football players to the Rose Bowl in 1954. The company also purchased advertisements in many of the Pasadena football teams' programs. (Courtesy of PMH, Hawkins Collection.)

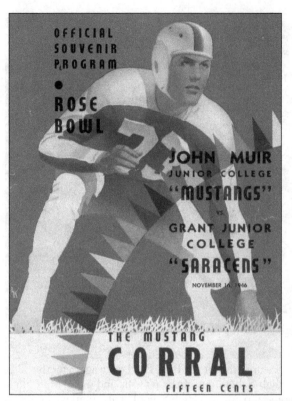

These programs from the 1940s are from the junior colleges that played their football games at the Rose Bowl. For decades, Pasadena teams that played each other in the same league shared the same home field. Community support was also shared by all of the teams. In every program, numerous pages are filled with advertisements placed by local businesses. Foster's Freeze, Powerline Self Service Station, and Coca-Cola all placed full-page ads in the junior colleges' programs.

Pasadena's high school football teams received similar support. In the 1950s and 1960s, Natzel Oldsmobile, Fishers restaurant, and Arnold's Jewelry Store were among the businesses that supported the high schools. Some companies' advertisements could be seen in the programs of multiple rival schools. These businesses were doing more than supporting particular teams; they were supporting all Pasadena athletes while marketing their products to Rose Bowl attendees.

The
RED & WHITE

20¢
OFFICIAL
SOUVENIR
PROGRAM

PASADENA HIGH SCHOOL
VS.
GLENDALE HIGH SCHOOL

Blair High
vs.
Santa Monica

FRIDAY, NOVEMBER 28, 1969
ROSE BOWL
8.00 P.M.

The Viking

J. ALLEN HAWKINS   November 27, 1963
330 N. Lake Ave
Pasadena, Calif.

Brother Al:
          On Tuesday December 10 th Pasadena Lodge will
hold its annual Football Awards night. The following
schools will be present for the program. Pasadena City
College team, coaches and Athletic director, Pasadena H.S.
coaches and their most valuable player, Muir H.S. coaches
and their most valuable player and St Francis H.S. coaches
and their most valuable player. We also expect Miss Jr Rose
Bowl and members of the Junior Chamber to be our guests
for that evening.I would appreciate if you would be on
hand to take pictures for our annual report to the grand
Lodge. Cocktails will be served at 6:30 p.m. followed by
dinner at 7:00 p.m. be our guest.

                              Fraternally yours

                              Ed Ransom

                              Youth Activity Chairman
P.S.
If you have any pictures of this past Babe Ruth season
sure would like to have them for the report.
                              Ed.

Professional photographer J. Allen Hawkins helped preserve many memorable people, places, and events in Pasadena's history. It is not surprising that the Elks Lodge requested his services in 1963 when the group honored all of Pasadena's football stars from Pasadena City College as well as Pasadena High School and John Muir High School (all of whom had played on the Rose Bowl field) at its annual football awards night. This event brought together rival players and coaches for an evening of camaraderie and entertaining awards. The guest list also included members of the Junior Chamber of Commerce and Miss Junior Rose Bowl. By mid-December, the Jaycees would be in the midst of their own festivities for the Junior Rose Bowl, as would Hawkins, who photographed the junior college championship and many of its accompanying festivities. (Courtesy of PMH, Hawkins Collection.)

Six

THE COMMUNITY'S BOWL

From its founding, Pasadena has always been a civic-minded community. The Rose Bowl, as a member of that community, has done its part by providing a large space for local events and gatherings. In addition to football games and concerts, Pasadenans have come to the bowl for graduations, flea markets, and car shows. The large stadium also made it possible for a group of residents to bring the Army-Navy game to Pasadena. Many people visit the stadium daily to simply walk, jog, or bike around the Rose Bowl loop. The Rose Bowl has also been the venue of choice for various charity and children's events.

The Rose Bowl is more than a gathering place—it is an icon in the Pasadena community. Businesses and organizations recognize the benefits of being associated with the stadium that has come to represent Pasadena to so many.

On any given morning, one can drive by the Rose Bowl and see dozens of Pasadenans jogging, walking, rollerblading, or bicycling around it. The famous stadium has become the local track. Although there is no actual Rose Bowl track, there is a well-trodden path around the perimeter of the bowl. (Photograph by Nancy Neuman-Bauer. Courtesy of PMH, PSN Collection.)

The Rose Bowl had become such a popular location for joggers and bicyclists that in 1993 one journalist for the *Pasadena Star-News* stated, "There is talk of closing the roads around the Rose Bowl to car traffic." Cyclists riding in packs were making it difficult for vehicles to navigate the Arroyo Seco streets. (Courtesy of PMH, PSN Collection.)

Put on by R. G. Canning Attractions, the Rose Bowl Flea Market is often advertised as an "olde tyme flea market" with traditional clowns and a high-wheel bicycle often just outside its gates. In this endearing photograph, taken in November 1980, a clown is out around Pasadena advertising that in addition to the regularly scheduled flea market, an additional flea market would be held on the third weekend of the month as well. Perhaps the extra flea market was added to encourage holiday shoppers to come to the bowl. The clown is holding a poster featuring the variety of antiques and collectables that could be found. Since the flea market features one-of-a-kind items, many bargain hunters pay the VIP admission price for an entrance to a special preview held hours before the flea market opens to the general public. (Courtesy of PMH, PSN Negatives Collection.)

The local bazaar boasts more than 2,500 vendors, with as many as 20,000 shoppers coming each month to view their wares. In addition to the usual swap-meet finds, numerous antique pieces can be found at bargain rates. The uniqueness of the objects available for sale is probably a contributing factor to the popularity of the flea market, which has been a Pasadena mainstay for more than 40 years. In addition to local bargain hunters, the flea market claims actors Clint Eastwood, Whoopi Goldberg, George Hamilton, and Ashley Olsen; singers Madonna, Cher, and Gwen Stefani; comedian Rob Schneider; and first lady of California Maria Shriver as VIP shoppers. (Above, courtesy of PHM, PSN Collection; below, courtesy of PMH, PSN Negatives Collection.)

A photograph similar to this one was used for a 1975 postcard. The fact that postcards were made featuring the Rose Bowl flea market tells anyone in doubt that this is no run-of-the-mill swap meet. The back of the postcard claims that "over a million items go on sale." (Courtesy of PMH, PSN Collection.)

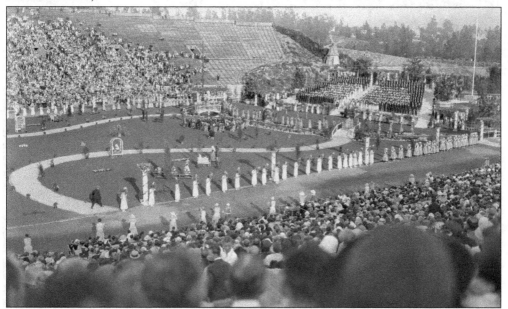

Early school graduation ceremonies at the Rose Bowl were filled with pageantry. Like the Tournament of Roses parades, each graduation had a theme. Note the benches, columns, bridge, and windmill that were brought in for this ceremony, which took place in June 1924. (Courtesy of PMH, Flag Collection.)

The graduation ceremonies at the Rose Bowl required organization and rehearsal. Three schools were involved in the 1959 mass graduation. Out of the 4,953 Pasadena students graduating that year, nearly 3,000 would be at the Rose Bowl: 800 from Pasadena High School, 716 from John Muir High School, and 1,233 from Pasadena City College. (Photograph by J. Allen Hawkins; courtesy of PMH, Hawkins Collection.)

After this graduation ceremony in 1977, there was talk that the graduations would be split. Some Pasadenans wanted Pasadena High School and Muir High School to have separate ceremonies rather than one large graduation at the Rose Bowl. There was enough opposition that the proposal was rejected. (Courtesy of PMH, PSN Negatives Collection.)

In 1951, all of the city's school marching bands joined together for a collaborative performance at the Rose Bowl. The seven bands marched together as separate letters to form the word "America." Nationalist themes were popular among the schools of patriotic Pasadena, and a sizable crowd gathered at the Rose Bowl to see the musical show. (Photograph by J. Allen Hawkins; courtesy of PMH, Hawkins Collection.)

Thirty years after the "America" performance, bands continued to regularly march on the Rose Bowl field. This photograph shows the band from Pasadena City College (PCC) practicing for a show. This particular performance was another example of a collaborative effort. Younger Pasadena students joined the PCC band on the field. (Courtesy of PMH, PSN Negatives Collection.)

These attendees are gathered at one of the first Easter Sunday services at the Rose Bowl in the 1920s. The fence that closed off the stadium when it was still a horseshoe shape can be seen behind the north-facing display. In later years, sunrise services were regularly held at the Rose Bowl.

The 21st annual Easter sunrise service, held on April 6, 1969, at the Rose Bowl, was a community affair. The Pasadena Association of Evangelicals, Pasadena City College, and the Salvation Army all participated in the event, which drew 2,500 people to the stadium. (Photograph by Richard Drew; courtesy of PMH, PSN Collection.)

During the bicentennial in 1976, the Rose Bowl played host to a car show in its parking lot. A number of vintage automobiles were on display, including an antique roadster. Fans also gathered around a 1937 Ford V-8 DeLuxe Club Cabriolet, a somewhat rare find and a favorite among hotrodders. This Club Cabriolet, along with the Woody next to it and many other vehicles on the "Rose Bowl showroom," were available for sale at the car show. In 1937, the Club Cabriolet would have sold for $760; today one can sell for more than $50,000. (Above, courtesy of PMH, PSN Collection; below, courtesy of PMH, PSN Negatives Collection.)

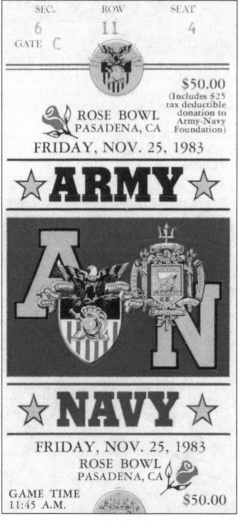

The Army-Navy game has been taking place annually since 1890. Most of these games have taken place in Philadelphia, but 9,000 West Point and Annapolis cadets came to Pasadena in 1983. A group of Pasadenans, many of whom had been involved with the Tournament of Roses, had formed the Army-Navy '83 Foundation with the express purpose of bringing the game to the Rose Bowl. Once the game was secured, the group of local citizens made all of the preparations. In addition to the game logistics, there was also the entertainment factor. Not surprisingly, weeklong festivities, which were described by journalist Jack Clary as "fittingly enough for Pasadena," included a parade featuring the Annapolis and West Point corps.

Between traveling entertainers and Fourth of July celebrations, the Rose Bowl has seen quite a few clowns and circus acts. As part of a philanthropic community, the Rose Bowl has also played host to a number of fund-raisers. In the spring of 1955, a local chapter of the Boy Scouts, located at 939 East Union Street in Pasadena, chose the Rose Bowl as the venue for its charity event. Perhaps inspired by other Rose Bowl entertainments, the young boys chose to put on a circus to raise money for their organization. All of the publicity photographs featured the south end of the Rose Bowl in the background. (Both, courtesy of PMH, Hawkins Collection.)

Earl Flanders posed in front of the Rose Bowl with his motorcycle a year after starting Flanders Motorcycle Accessories with his wife, Lucile. Taken by a professional photographer, the image was most likely used for advertising. The company, like the Rose Bowl, remains a Pasadena fixture to this day, operating at 340 South Fair Oaks Avenue. (Courtesy of PMH, Hawkins Collection.)

The Astros were the 1966 Rose Bowl Colt League all-stars. Although baseball was not played in the Rose Bowl, the league that played in the nearby park was still named after the community stadium. The aquatic center, a later addition to Brookside Park, also bears the bowl's name. (Courtesy of PMH, Hawkins Collection.)

Seven

THE INTERNATIONAL BOWL

By making the focus of the after-parade festivities football, the Tournament of Roses Association was hoping to make the Rose Bowl and its New Year's Day festivities an international phenomenon. Although the Rose Parade and game are known worldwide, nothing put Pasadena and the Rose Bowl on the global map faster than hosting international sporting events. During the 1932 Olympics in Los Angeles, the Rose Bowl served as the track for the cycling events. Then, in the 1984 Olympic games, the Rose Bowl played host to a different kind of football—soccer. The soccer games continued with the World Cup in 1994 and the Women's World Cup in 1999. Smaller international youth matches have also been held at the Rose Bowl.

These games ensured that Pasadena and the Rose Bowl received substantial international attention. Dedicated fans from around the world came to cheer on their nations' top athletes. Visitors from Brazil, Italy, Sweden, Bulgaria, Columbia, Romania, and several other countries joined American sports fans in the stands. The Rose Bowl's exposure was further enhanced because it had the honor of holding the all-important final games for the 1994 World Cup, probably because it was the largest of the nine American venues. In addition to the lucky thousands who were able to acquire seats, millions more tuned in to watch the games on television. The Women's World Cup finals, held a few years later, were also well attended. The Rose Bowl's relationship with the Fédération Internationale de Football Association (FIFA), the governing body for soccer, has continued into 2010, making it a truly international bowl.

These are tickets to various events held during the 1932 Olympics. Aside from the Long Beach Marine Stadium, which was the only place suitable for the rowing competition, Pasadena's Rose Bowl was the only venue, aside from the Olympic Stadium in Los Angeles, to play host to an Olympic event. (Photograph by Harry Scheibel; courtesy of PMH, PSN Collection.)

In 1932, Los Angeles hosted the Summer Olympics, and Pasadena's Rose Bowl held the four track cycling events (which were still for men only). The cost to see one of these races at the Rose Bowl was $2 per person. After the Olympics ended and the bicycle track was dismantled, the lumber was used for the La Casita del Arroyo Clubhouse.

In July 1984, workers laid down new sod in preparation for the Olympic football (soccer) matches. The new field was laid down five days before the first match at the Rose Bowl took place. During the course of the Olympics, teams from 10 different countries played 11 games at the Rose Bowl. (Photograph by Walt Mancini; courtesy of PMH, PSN Collection.)

This fence had been placed around the Rose Bowl during the Olympics for security purposes. Crown Fencing employees removed the fence after the Olympic soccer finals were over. The man rolling up the fencing is wearing an official Olympic baseball cap. (Photograph by Walt Mancini; courtesy of PMH, PSN Collection.)

These "LA 84" banners were part of a project to prepare for the Olympics. Hundreds of banners like these, along with flags from the 16 nations participating in the soccer matches, were hung around the Rose Bowl. In addition to the banners and flags, extra attention was given to the landscaping, and parts of the stadium were repainted. (Photograph by Walt Mancini; courtesy of PMH, PSN Collection.)

The iconic mascot of the 1984 Los Angeles Olympic Games was a character known as Sam the Eagle. Sam came to Pasadena to congratulate the Olympic soccer players at the Rose Bowl. The giant cartoon-like eagle also drew a crowd of local children to the stadium. (Photograph by Walt Mancini; courtesy of PMH, PSN Collection.)

American spectators cheered on the U.S. soccer team as they played Italy during the 1984 Summer Olympics. This was the only game at the Rose Bowl that the American team played. Unfortunately, Italy beat the United States 1-0, and the U.S. team did not make it to the quarter finals. (Courtesy of PMH, PSN Collection.)

Here is a glimpse of what the Rose Bowl looked like after the Olympics left town. Although there was much work to be done, there was only a short time in which to do it. The Olympics were over, but UCLA's football season was getting ready to start its third season at the bowl in less than a month.

After playing host to two Olympic events at the Rose Bowl, Pasadena's interest and involvement in the Olympics continued into the 21st century. In 2002, when the Winter Olympic Games were in Salt Lake City, Utah, the Olympic Torch came down the streets of Pasadena. Velma Dunn Ploessel, a 1936 Olympian, carried the torch through the city.

One reason soccer fans may have had trouble getting seats at the World Cup was that there were fewer seats available. In July 1993, crews ripped out seats in the Rose Bowl to make room for a soccer field for the upcoming World Cup finals. The transformation cost the stadium (and fans) more than 10,000 seats. (Courtesy of PMH, PSN Collection.)

Pasadena once again received international attention when the Rose Bowl played host to the World Cup in 1994; however, the sign at the entrance to the Rose Bowl read "World Cup XV–Los Angeles." The Pasadena City Council was incensed and ordered the sign to be removed since the World Cup was taking place in Pasadena, not Los Angeles. (Photograph by Scott Quintard; courtesy of PMH, PSN Collection.)

When the Rose Bowl played host to the World Cup, the local arts community also got involved. The World Cup mural project was located on the top front section of the Armory Center for the Arts building, at 145 North Raymond Avenue. This homemade mural for the World Cup made it clear to visitors that they were in the city of Pasadena. (Photograph by Walt Mancini; courtesy of PMH, PSN Collection.)

Like other major events at the Rose Bowl, the 1994 World Cup was preceded by a parade down Colorado Boulevard. For the "Pasadena Welcomes the World" parade, a group of children dressed up to represent different countries. Pictured is the Italian representative, Claire Carlstroem. (Photograph by Lisa McCarthy; courtesy of PMH, PSN Collection.)

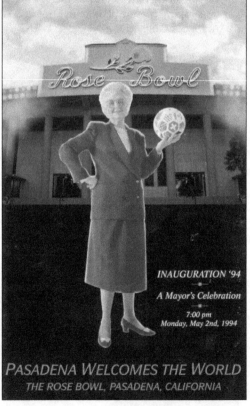

INAUGURATION '94

A Mayor's Celebration

7:00 pm
Monday, May 2nd, 1994

PASADENA WELCOMES THE WORLD
THE ROSE BOWL, PASADENA, CALIFORNIA

Pasadena mayor Katie Nack had more than one reason to celebrate in May 1994. Nack threw a free celebration after she was unanimously voted the new mayor by the city council. The mayor had good reason to hold her party at the Rose Bowl since the upcoming World Cup games were expected to bring in substantial revenue for the city.

Traveling from Porto Alegre, Rio Grande do Sul, Brazil, Clovis Fernades came to Pasadena with his son to see his fifth World Cup match. Fernades was confident that Brazil would win, and he was not disappointed. Brazil beat out Bulgaria, Sweden, and Italy to take its fourth championship title. (Photograph by Walt Mancini; courtesy of PMH, PSN Collection.)

The downside of international popularity was that locals had trouble getting tickets to see the World Cup at the Rose Bowl. These Dexter Corporation employees both applied for tickets. Seamus Gillespie (left), seen smiling with his tickets, had his name drawn, while Gabriel Casas was not so lucky. (Photograph by Joe Messinger; courtesy of PMH, PSN Collection.)

In 1999, the Rose Bowl was one of eight American stadiums to hold the FIFA Women's World Cup. Like the World Cup five years prior, Pasadena had the honor of hosting the final game, which broke attendance records for the sport with more than 90,000 spectators at the Rose Bowl to see Brandi Chastain and the U.S. team claim victory over China. (Photograph by Brett Whitesell; courtesy of isiphotos.com.)

Although it was an international competition, the two teams in the Disney International Youth Soccer Cup 1994 women's finals were the Pasadena Flyers and the Arcadia Dream Team. Right after the game ended in sudden death overtime, Rachel Trishe, who scored the winning goal, was immediately dog piled by her team. The disappointed player in the background is Arcadia goalkeeper Tina Thompson. (Photograph by Lisa McCarthy; courtesy of PMH, PSN Collection.)

Eight

OTHER TRACKS AND FIELDS

When the Tournament of Roses Association originally built the Rose Bowl, it had intended that the stadium only be used for one particular sport—American football. Throughout the years, however, various athletic events have been played at the stadium in the Arroyo Seco against the objections of neighbors and pigskin purists. In addition to football, the Rose Bowl has played host to soccer matches, marathons, and track-and-field meets. Slightly less traditional activities have included rodeos, Frisbee championships, and flying small airplanes over the field. And despite opposition, the famous football field has even accommodated automobiles for midget car and motocross racing. Some of these non-football activities were so well loved by the community that for a few years they, too, were considered a Rose Bowl tradition.

For every event held at the Rose Bowl, the venue was transformed. Mounds of dirt, clay, hay, and whatever else was needed were brought in by the truckload—in some cases, 700 truckloads. These transformations were impressive not just in scale, but in quality. The new tracks and fields that were laid down always drew praise among that particular sport's community. Yet no matter how well constructed, these new tracks and fields rarely remained. They were built up only to be demolished when the field needed to be readied for football season. Football is the stadium's main sporting event, but it is certainly not the only one.

This medal and trophy were for the Rose Bowl Invitational track-and-field meet, which was held to commemorate the installation of the stadium's new track. The first annual meet was in 1966 and was sponsored by the Junior Chamber of Commerce. At a luncheon for the event, *Pasadena Star-News* writer Rube Samuelson said, "It was here that the famous Notre Dame Four Horsemen made their last ride. But it was also here that some of the events, notably cycling, were held in connection with the 1932 Olympic Games. This track may be the beginning of a rosy era for sports competition." The track was dedicated to the youth of Pasadena. (Photographs by J. Allen Hawkins; courtesy of PMH, Hawkins Collection.)

In 1978, the Rose Bowl marathon drew runners from all over Southern California to Pasadena. The record setter for the best overall time, Ben Wilson (pictured here), was from Claremont. Other athletes with the fastest times were from as nearby as Glendale and as far away as Bakersfield and Laguna Beach. Today the Rose Bowl plays host to half marathons, 10Ks, 5Ks, and children's runs. Many participants see other Pasadena landmarks on the course, including the Colorado Street Bridge and Devil's Gate Dam. Unlike in 1978, the finish line for today's races is inside the stadium on the field. (Courtesy of PMH, PSN Negatives Collection.)

The *Pasadena Star-News* caption for this 1992 photograph read, "With a 1st place time of 43.05, three time Rose Bowl triathlon winner Larry Rhoades finishes the 3 mile run, and heads toward his bike to ride 10 miles, after which he and approximately 400 other triathlon contestants will swim 400 meters at the Rose Bowl Aquatics Center." (Photograph by Nancy Newman; courtesy of PMH, PSN Collection.)

On September 8, 1979, the first 50-kilometer bicycle race ended at the Rose Bowl. Although most participants were in bicycling gear, the race was more of a festive event than a competition. The event drew families and young and old alike. The 2,000 entries even included a bicycle built for two. (Courtesy of PMH, PSN Negatives Collection.)

In 1946, dirt and racing clay were laid down in the Rose Bowl to create a new track for midget auto racing. Although the event was opposed by the Tournament of Roses, the races were supported by other local organizations as well as by many residents. The Rose Bowl broke the U.S. attendance record for the sport on the first night of racing with an attendance count of 65,000. (Photograph by J. Allen Hawkins; courtesy of PMH, Hawkins Collection.)

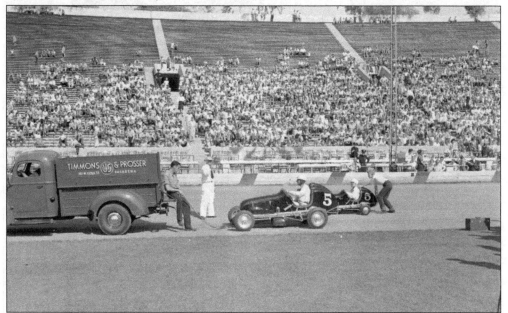

Like any race, the midget races at the Rose Bowl were not without crashes, fires, and other car problems. At this race, the No. 5 race car was assisted off of the track by Timmons and Prosser U.S. Tires. In 1946, the company was located at 161 West Colorado Street. The business is still in Pasadena today, operating on Foothill Boulevard. (Photograph by J. Allen Hawkins; courtesy of PMH, Hawkins Collection.)

Just like the Fourth of July celebrations at the Rose Bowl, the midget auto races also had clowns to entertain the crowd. This clown seems to be having a problem with his decorative racing car. Although the midget auto races were popular, this clown performed for a relatively small crowd. (Photograph by J. Allen Hawkins; courtesy of PMH, Hawkins Collection.)

Fans at a 1946 Rose Bowl auto race surrounded one of the drivers as he relaxed on the tailgate of his support vehicle. Note the cans of motor oil, spare tires, and other auto maintenance supplies in the back of the Woody. (Photograph by J. Allen Hawkins; courtesy of PMH, Hawkins Collection.)

In 1983, Pasadena hosted its first Superbowl of Motocross, but the event almost did not make it to the Rose Bowl. A city ordinance prohibited motorized racing in the Arroyo Seco, and many residents were opposed to the races. After much debate (three city directors voted against hosting the event), the races were approved, and the Rose Bowl was once again transformed. (Photograph by Ed Norgard; courtesy of PMH, PSN Collection.)

More than dirt was needed to convert the Rose Bowl football field into a motocross raceway. This photograph at right shows workers installing the hydro barricades that were put in place before the 1987 races. The hydro barricades replaced the stacks of straw that were used in previous years for other races. (Photograph by Andrew Taylor; courtesy of PMH, PSN Collection.)

Although many Arroyo Seco neighbors continued to complain about the noise and air pollution every year, the races continued and were declared "an annual Pasadena tradition" by *Pasadena Star-News*. Approximately 700 truckloads of dirt were brought in to convert the football field into a racing track for Mickey Thompson's Championship Grand Prix in 1989. Plastic and plywood protected the field underneath. (Photograph by Walt Mancini; courtesy of PMH, PSN Collection.)

A variety of sporting events have taken place at the Rose Bowl, which may be why in May 1980 one *Pasadena Star-News* photographer mistakenly thought that the athletes whom he was photographing might have been playing rugby. Although the subject of this photograph was in fact kicking a football, rugby would not have been out of the question on this versatile field. (Courtesy of PMH, PSN Negatives Collection.)

Although chariot races were never staged at the Rose Bowl on New Year's Day, races did take place at the Rose Bowl Rodeo in 1965 in honor of the races at Tournament Park. The program reads, "Casey has made arrangements for a chariot race featuring the original Ben Hur Horses used in the multi-million dollar Metro-Goldwyn-Mayer motion picture."

CASEY TIBBS'
FIRST ANNUAL

ROSE BOWL
RODEO

THE LARGEST SINGLE DAY RODEO EVENT IN THE WORLD FEATURING TOP COWBOYS FROM ALL OVER THE COUNTRY ■ PLUS MANY STARS OF MOTION PICTURES AND TV ■ TWO SPECIAL RACING EVENTS ■ THE ANNUAL ROSE BOWL DERBY IN WHICH THE NATION'S TOP JOCKEYS RACE BURROS ■ AND A CHARIOT RACE FEATURING THE HORSES FROM THE MOVIE "BEN HUR."

1965

The photograph below shows the diversity of the Rose Bowl. Converted for a rodeo in 1983, the stadium barely resembles the football field for which it is famous. Although only half of the stadium is being used, the Rose Bowl still held tens of thousands of rodeo spectators. (Photograph by Tom La Barbera; courtesy of PMH, PSN Collection.)

The rodeos continued at the Rose Bowl into the 1980s. This photograph, taken in 1983, shows an unidentified rider participating in the saddle-bronc competition. The goal of this event is to stay on the bronco for as long as possible without being thrown. Some animal rights groups opposed the rodeos, claiming that they were cruel to the animals. After much debate, the Pasadena City Council banned the events on city-owned properties, including the Rose Bowl, in 2001 by a 6-1 vote. The ordinance, which also prohibited circuses, required organizations wanting to perform with animals to get prior approval from the Pasadena Humane Society. Equestrian groups participating in the Tournament of Roses Parade were exempt from the ordinance, along with cat and dog shows. Pasadena was one of the first cities in the state to pass a law regulating animal entertainment. (Courtesy of PMH, PSN Collection.)

Sponsored by Wham-O, a company that manufactures Frisbees and other recreational products, the World Frisbee Championships brought a new sport to the Rose Bowl. There was also a Junior World Frisbee Championship and even a Frisbee Dog World Championship. Today Frisbee championships are truly worldwide, with international participants and venues.

In 1976, two 19-year-olds took the title of World Frisbee Champion. They were Peter Bloeme and Monika Lou. People came from around the country to compete in the Rose Bowl competition. Lou was from Berkeley, California, and Bloeme was from New York, New York. (Photograph by Vanguard Photography; courtesy of PMH.)

In 1976, the Frisbee Dog World Championship was held in conjunction with the World Frisbee Championship. No ordinary dog, Ashley Whippet was world famous for his Frisbee-catching and won the championship three years in a row. Whippet came back to the Rose Bowl the following year to perform at Super Bowl XI. (Photograph by Vanguard Photography; courtesy of PMH.)

The object in the air to the left of the scoreboard is not a Frisbee, but a "minny jet." This photograph, taken in 1946, shows the small, remote-controlled airplane being flown around the Rose Bowl stadium. Decades later, the Pasadena Soaring Society, founded in 1973, would also fly radio-controlled sailplanes on the Rose Bowl lawn. (Photograph by J. Allen Hawkins; courtesy of PMH, Hawkins Collection.)

Nine

THE SUPER BOWL

The New Year's Day Rose Bowl is known as one of the biggest, if not the biggest, bowl game in college football. The professionals have their own big game. Every winter, the champion of the National Football Conference plays the champion of the American Football League for the honor of being crowned the winner of the National Football League's (NFL) Super Bowl. The NFL game's popularity is so great that companies are willing to pay millions of dollars for a 30-second advertisement.

The Rose Bowl has played host to the Super Bowl despite having never been the home of an NFL team. It is one of only two stadiums in the country to have done so, and it has done it five times. In 1977, the Oakland Raiders took on the Minnesota Vikings; in 1980, the Pittsburgh Steelers beat the Los Angeles Rams; in 1983, the Washington Redskins upset the favored Miami Dolphins; in 1987, the New York Giants beat the Denver Broncos; and in 1993, the Dallas Cowboys crushed the Buffalo Bills. Some players and fans undoubtedly have fonder memories of Pasadena than others, but none of them can argue with the fact that the weather was perfect. The conditions were ideal for every game; it was sunny and between 61 and 74 degrees on all five winter days.

As this photograph illustrates, the Rose Bowl was packed for Super Bowl XI, but far more than the 103,438 in attendance saw the game. The Nielsen rating for this game was over 44 percent, which meant that almost half of the television viewers that day were watching the Raiders take on the Vikings in Pasadena. (Courtesy of PMH, PSN Collection.)

When most people think of Shirley Temple and the Rose Bowl, they think of the adorable movie star who was the Rose Parade grand marshal in 1939 and again in 1989. However, in 1977, another Shirley Temple from North Plain, New Jersey, came to the Rose Bowl to cheer on the Raiders at Super Bowl XI. (Photograph by Walt Mancini; courtesy of PMH, PSN Collection.)

Pictured are Minnesota Vikings fans before the 1977 Super Bowl. These fans were probably not as excited later in the day, as the Oakland Raiders beat the Vikings 32-14 to win their first Super Bowl. At least fans from Minnesota got to enjoy Pasadena's famous January weather; it was 74 degrees and sunny. (Photograph by Mark Denton; courtesy of PMH, PSN Collection.)

Vikings mascot Hub Meeds revved up the crowd during the big game. Meed told the *Ocala Star-Banner* that years ago he and his brother had attended Minnesota's first Super Bowl dressed in Viking costumes. After that game, Meed approached the Vikings about being their mascot and went on to represent the team during the 1970s and 1980s. (Photograph by Robert Paz; courtesy of PMH, PSN Collection.)

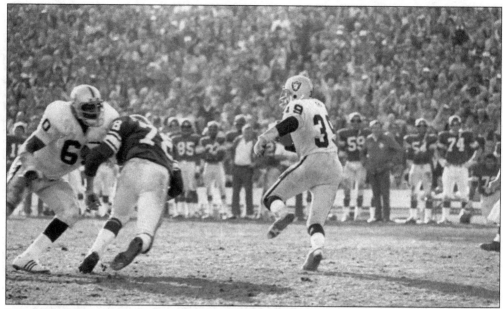

Super Bowl XI was the first Super Bowl in which the No. 1 team from the American Football Conference and the No. 1 team from the National Football Conference made the competition. The Raiders were the favorite by a narrow margin. By the end of the game, this offensive lineman's team scored more than twice as many points as the Vikings. (Courtesy of PMH, PSN Negatives Collection.)

Super Bowl XIV was held less than three weeks after the big Rose Bowl Game in 1980. This photograph shows just some of the preparations for the big day. All of these snack vendors and lights would definitely be needed when the 100,000-strong crowd came to the stadium. (Courtesy of PMH, PSN Negatives Collection.)

Many fans congregated in Brookside Park before big games. Here Pittsburgh Steelers fans watch as one of their own demonstrates a punt kick. This fan had reason to be so exuberant. With quarterback Terry Bradshaw, the Steelers were the strong favorite, and they ultimately won Super Bowl XIV 31-19. (Courtesy of PMH, PSN Collection.)

These Rams fans are participating in some low-key tailgating before Super Bowl XIV. Los Angeles fans did not have to travel far to see the game since the Rose Bowl was only 18 miles away from the Rams home stadium. Unfortunately, this was the team's only appearance at a Rose Bowl Super Bowl. (Courtesy of PMH, PSN Collection.)

Marketing used an alternate approach in 1983. Unlike the ticket to the 1977 Super Bowl, which featured a rose, mountains, and a stadium that resembled the Rose Bowl, these tickets for Super Bowl XVII had a very different look. Although played at the Rose Bowl, the building on the ticket resembles a Hollywood movie theater. (Photograph by John Lloyd; courtesy of PMH, PSN Collection.)

In 1983, "killer bees" descended on the Rose Bowl for Super Bowl XVII. The Miami Dolphin's defense had six players with last names starting with the letter "B." Pictured are fans Steve McMann (left) and Jim McCourt (right), who dressed like bees to show their support for defensive tackle Bob Baumhower and the other Miami Killer Bees. (Photograph by John Lloyd; courtesy of PMH, PSN Collection.)

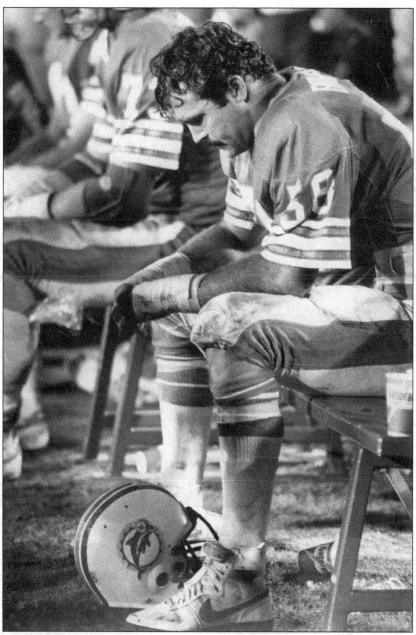

In 1983, many football enthusiasts mistakenly thought that Miami's defensive line would give the team the advantage they needed to win the Super Bowl. Despite being the favorite to win, the Dolphins lost Super Bowl XVII to the Washington Redskins 27-17. Pictured is one of Miami's Killer Bees, linebacker Kim Bokamper. This photograph was taken at the end of the game. Earlier in the game, Bokamper had lost the ball to Redskin quarterback Joe Theismann right after successfully blocking Theismann's pass. It was the fourth Super Bowl for the Dolphins and the first for Bokamper. His second Super Bowl with the Dolphins, just two years later, was played at another California college stadium—Stanford Stadium in Northern California. The Rose Bowl and Stanford Stadium are the only stadiums to hold Super Bowls while never being the home field of an NFL team. (Courtesy of PMH, PSN Collection.)

Workers laid down new sod in preparation for Super Bowl XXI in 1987, when the New York Giants defeated the Denver Broncos 39-20. Pasadena had won the bid from other competing cities in Southern California and across the country. Looking at this photograph, it is easy to see why the NFL owners voted for the picturesque stadium. The Rose Bowl was on television for months after the game as the backdrop for Disney's first "I'm going to Disney World!" television advertisement, which featured MVP Phil Simms. The Giants quarterback contributed to a few Super Bowl firsts that day. He was named MVP after setting the record for highest completion percentage in a Super Bowl. He also set a new record for NFL postseason games, with a completion percentage of 88 percent (22 out of 25 passes completed). That record remained unbroken for more than two decades. (Photograph by Walt Mancini; courtesy of PMH, PSN Collection.)

Vendor Inman Jones displayed his souvenirs that were for sale for the 1987 Super Bowl. That year's Super Bowl logo featured a large stylized red rose, making it clear where the game was being held. Pasadena had known it would be hosting Super Bowl XXI since 1983. (Photograph by Ed Norgord; courtesy of PMH, PSN Collection.)

These tickets for Super Bowl XXI also featured the iconic red rose. The Rose Bowl played host to its fifth and last Super Bowl five years later in 1993. With no professional football teams currently in the Los Angeles area, it is unknown if the NFL's biggest game will return to the Rose Bowl. (Photograph by Ed Norgard; courtesy of PMH, PSN Collection.)

After the NFL decided to pull Super Bowl XXVII out of Arizona, the Rose Bowl was given the honor of having the 1993 Super Bowl. This photograph shows crews preparing for the tailgate party for Buffalo Bills fans. The Bills would lose to the Dallas Cowboys 52-17. (Courtesy of PMH, PSN Collection.)

Sam Estrada bought this football cap for his son Simon from the Footlocker tent at the 1993 game. The cap was for the San Francisco 49ers. Vendors at the Super Bowl offered souvenirs supporting a variety of teams, including California teams not playing in that year's big game. (Photograph by Walt Mancini; courtesy of PMH, PSN Collection.)

Despite the fact that the New York Giants were the favorites to win, these Denver Bronco fans were still excited to come to Pasadena and watch their team play in Super Bowl XXI. Although their team lost, they got to see Denver's Louis Wright, Steve Foley, and Tom Jackson, play in their last game before all three retired. (Photograph by John Lloyd; courtesy of PMH, PSN Collection.)

In Pasadena, big football games tend to be accompanied by celebrations down Colorado Boulevard. Super Bowl XXVII was no exception. Many fans, such as Tim Buchanan of Buffalo, New York, could be seen cheering at the Superfest Celebration the day before the big game. The spirit of the events that take place in the Rose Bowl always enlivens the entire city. (Photograph by Paul Morse; courtesy of PMH, PSN Collection.)

Rose Bowl Scores
Since 1923

1923	USC 14, Penn State 3
1924	Washington 14, Navy 14
1925	Notre Dame 27, Stanford 10
1926	Alabama 20, Washington 19
1927	Stanford 7, Alabama 7
1928	Stanford 7, Pittsburgh 6
1929	Georgia Tech 8, California 7
1930	USC 47, Pittsburgh 14
1931	Alabama 24, Washington State 0
1932	USC 21, Tulane 12
1933	USC 35, Pittsburgh 0
1934	Columbia 7, Stanford 0
1935	Alabama 29, Stanford 13
1936	Stanford 7, Southern Methodist University 0
1937	Pittsburgh 21, Washington 0
1938	California 13, Alabama 0
1939	USC 7, Duke 3
1940	USC 14, Tennessee 0
1941	Stanford 21, Nebraska 13
1942	Oregon State 20, Duke 16*
1943	Georgia 9, UCLA 0
1944	USC 29, Washington 0
1945	USC 25, Tennessee 0
1946	Alabama 34, USC 14
1947	Illinois 45, UCLA 14
1948	Michigan 49, USC 0
1949	Northwestern 20, California 14
1950	Ohio State 17, California 14
1951	Michigan 14, California 6
1952	Illinois 40, Stanford 7
1953	USC 7, Wisconsin 0
1954	Michigan State 28, UCLA 20
1955	Ohio State 20, USC 7
1956	Michigan State 17, UCLA 14
1957	Iowa 35, Oregon State 19
1958	Ohio State 10, Oregon 7
1959	Iowa 38, California 12
1960	Washington 44, Wisconsin 8
1961	Washington 17, Minnesota 7
1962	Minnesota 21, UCLA 3
1963	USC 42, Wisconsin 37
1964	Illinois 17, Washington 7
1965	Michigan 34, Oregon State 7
1966	UCLA 14, Michigan State 12

1967	Purdue 14, USC 13
1968	USC 14, Indiana 3
1969	Ohio State 27, USC 16
1970	USC 10, Michigan 3
1971	Stanford 27, Ohio State 17
1972	Stanford 13, Michigan 12
1973	USC 42, Ohio State 17
1974	Ohio State 42, USC 21
1975	USC 18, Ohio State 17
1976	UCLA 23, Ohio State 10
1977	USC 14, Michigan 6
1978	Washington 27, Michigan 20
1979	USC 17, Michigan 10
1980	USC 17, Ohio State 16
1981	Michigan 23, Washington 6
1982	Washington 28, Iowa 0
1983	UCLA 24, Michigan 14
1984	UCLA 45, Illinois 9
1985	USC 20, Ohio State 17
1986	UCLA 45, Iowa 28
1987	Arizona State 22, Michigan 15
1988	Michigan State 20, USC 17
1989	Michigan 22, USC 14
1990	USC 17, Michigan 10
1991	Washington 46, Iowa 34
1992	Washington 34, Michigan 14
1993	Michigan 38, Washington 31
1994	Wisconsin 21, UCLA 16
1995	Penn State 38, Oregon 20
1996	USC 41, Northwestern 32
1997	Ohio State 20, Arizona State 17
1998	Michigan 21, Washington State 16
1999	Wisconsin 38, UCLA 31
2000	Wisconsin 17, Stanford 9
2001	Washington 34, Purdue 24
2002	Miami 37, Nebraska 14**
2003	Oklahoma 34, Washington State 14
2004	USC 28, Michigan 14
2005	Texas 38, Michigan 37
2006	Texas 41, USC 38**
2007	USC 32, Michigan 18
2008	USC 49, Illinois 17
2009	USC 38, Penn State 24
2010	Ohio State 26, Oregon 17

SUPER BOWL SCORES
FOR GAMES PLAYED IN THE ROSE BOWL

1977	Oakland 32, Minnesota 14
1980	Pittsburgh 31, Los Angeles 19
1983	Washington 27, Miami 17
1987	New York (Giants) 39, Denver 20
1993	Dallas 52, Buffalo 17

* Game played in North Carolina
** Also a BCS Championship Game

Visit us at
arcadiapublishing.com